MARVELOUS Muffins, Breads, AND Pancakes

Kari Cornell Photographs by **Brie Cohen**

M MILLBROOK PRESS • MINNEAPOLIS

For my mom, who taught me how to experiment in the kitchen;
and for Will, Theo, and Brian, who cheerfully sampled every
muffin, bread, and pancake I put on the table —K.C.

For Tami and Brennan, for always making me pancakes —B.C.

Photography by Brie Cohen
Food in photographs prepared by chef David Vlach
Illustrations by Laura Westlund/Independent Picture Service
The image on page 5 is used with the permission of © iStockphoto.com/stuartbur.

Allergy alert: The recipes in this book contain ingredients to which some
people can be allergic. Anyone with food allergies or sensitivities should follow
the advice of a physician or other medical professional.

Millbrook Press
A division of Lerner Publishing Group, Inc.
241 First Avenue North
Minneapolis, MN 55401 U.S.A.

Website address: www.lernerbooks.com

Main body text set in Felbridge Std Regular 11/14.
Typeface provided by Monotype Typography.

Library of Congress Cataloging-in-Publication Data

Cornell, Kari A.
Marvelous muffins, breads, and pancakes /
by Kari Cornell ; photographs by Brie Cohen.
pages cm. — (You're the chef)
Includes index.
ISBN 978–0–7613–6636–2 (lib. bdg. : alk. paper)
ISBN 978–1–4677–1713–7 (eBook)
1. Muffins. 2. Cooking (Bread) 3. Breakfasts.
I. Cohen, Brie, illustrator. II. Title.
TX770.M83C67 2014
641.81'5—dc23   2012048927

Manufactured in the United States of America
1 – CG – 7/15/13

TABLE of CONTENTS

Are you ready to make some marvelous muffins, breads, and pancakes? YOU can be the chef and make food for yourself and your family. These easy recipes are perfect for a chef who is just learning to cook. And they're so delicious, you'll want to make them again and again!

I developed these recipes with the help of my kids, who are six and eight years old. They can't do all the cooking on their own yet, but they can do a lot.

Can't get enough of cooking? Check out www.lerneresource.com for bonus recipes, healthful eating tips, links to cooking technique videos, and more!

BEFORE YOU START

Reserve your space! Always ask for permission to work in the kitchen.

Find a helper! You will need an adult helper for some tasks. Talk with this person to decide what steps you can do on your own and what steps the adult will help with.

Make a plan! Read through the whole recipe before you start cooking. Do you have the ingredients you'll need? If you don't know what a certain ingredient is, see page 31 to find out more. Do you understand each step? If you don't understand a technique, such as *grease* or *slice*, turn to page 7. At the beginning of each recipe, you'll see how much time you'll need to prepare the recipe and to cook it. The recipe will also tell you how many servings it makes. Small drawings at the top of each recipe let you know what major kitchen equipment you'll need—such as a stovetop, a blender, or an oven.

stovetop

blender

knives

waffle iron

oven

Wash up! Always wash your hands with soap and water before you start cooking. And wash them again after you touch raw eggs, meat, or fish.

Get it together! Find the tools you'll use, such as measuring cups or a mixing bowl. Gather all the ingredients you'll need. That way you won't have to stop to look for things once you start cooking.

SAFETY TIPS

That's sharp! Your adult helper needs to be in the kitchen when you are using a knife, a grater, or a peeler. If you are doing the cutting, use a cutting board. Cut away from your body, and keep your fingers away from the blade.

That's hot! Be sure an adult is in the kitchen if you use the stove or the oven. Your adult helper can help you cook on the stove and take hot things out of the oven.

Tie it back! If you have long hair, tie it back or wear a hat. If you have long sleeves, roll them up. You want to keep your hair and clothing out of the food and away from flames or other heat sources.

Turn that handle! When cooking on the stove, turn the pot handle toward the back. That way, no one will accidentally bump the pot and knock it off the stove.

Wash it! If you are working with raw eggs or meat, you need to keep things extra clean. After cutting raw meat or fish, wash the knife and the cutting board right away. They must be clean before you use them to cut anything else.

Go slowly! Take your time when you're working. When you are doing something for the first time; such as peeling or grating, be sure not to rush.

Above all, have fun!

Finish the job right!

One of your most important jobs as a chef is to clean up when you're done. Wash the dishes with soap and warm water. Wipe off the countertop or the table. Put away any unused ingredients. The adults in your house will be more excited for you to cook next time if you take charge of cleaning up.

COOKING TOOLS

bowls

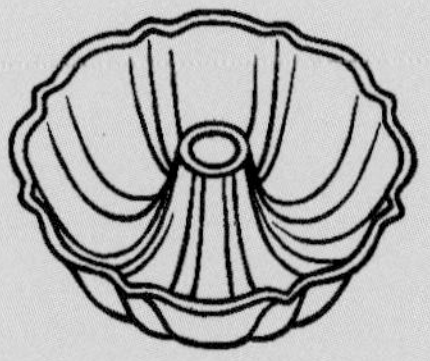

Bundt cake pan

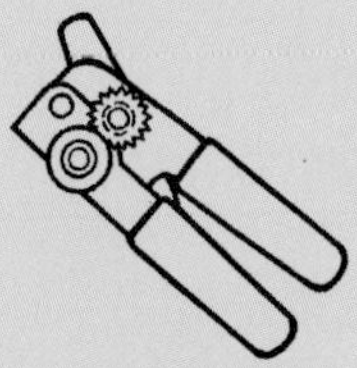

can opener

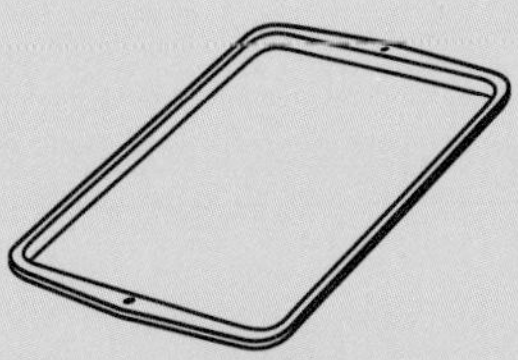

cookie sheet

cutting board

dry measuring cups

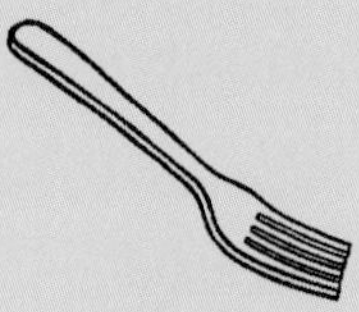

fork

frying pan

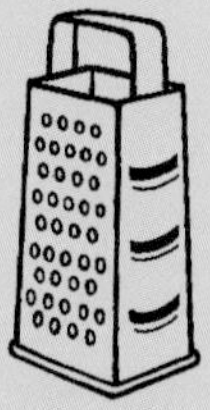

grater

knives

ladle

liquid measuring cup

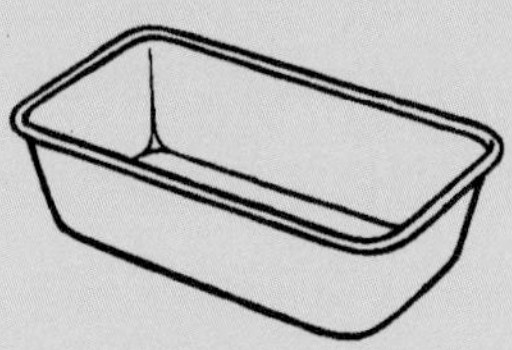

loaf pan

measuring spoons

muffin tin

oven mitt

pastry brush

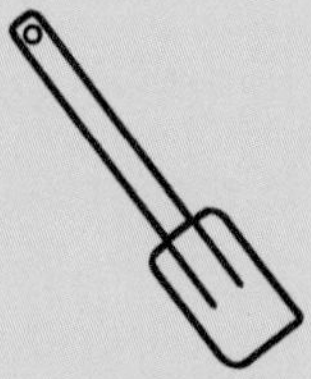

rubber scraper

saucepans

spatula

strainer

vegetable peeler

whisk

wire cooling rack

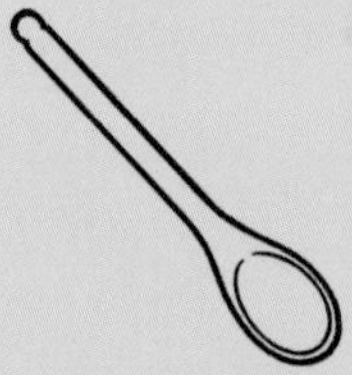

wooden spoon

TECHNIQUES

bake: to cook in the oven

blend: to stir together with a spoon, whisk, or blender until well mixed

boil: to heat liquid on a stovetop until it starts to bubble

chop: to cut food into small pieces using a knife

discard: to throw away or put in a compost bin. Discarded parts of fruits and vegetables and eggshells can be put in a compost bin, if you have one.

drain: to pour the liquid off a food. You can drain food by pouring it into a colander or a strainer. If you are draining water or juice from canned food, you can also use the lid to hold the food back while the liquid pours out.

grate: to use a food grater to shred food into small pieces

grease: to coat a pan in oil or butter so baked food won't stick to the bottom

mix: to stir food using a spoon or fork

preheat: to turn the oven to the temperature you will need for baking. An oven takes about 15 minutes to heat up.

puree: to blend until smooth

rise: to place dough in a warm place until doubled in size

set aside: to put nearby in a bowl or a plate or on a clean workspace

slice: to cut food into thin pieces

sprinkle: to scatter on top

whisk: to stir food quickly with a fork or a whisk

MEASURING

To measure **dry ingredients**, such as sugar or flour, spoon the ingredient into a measuring cup until it is full. Then use the back of a table knife to level it off. Do not pack it down unless the recipe tells you to. Do not use measuring cups made for liquids.

When you're measuring a **liquid**, such as milk or water, use a clear glass or plastic measuring cup. Set the cup on the table or a counter, and pour the liquid into the cup. Pour slowly and stop when the liquid has reached the correct line.

Don't measure your ingredients over the bowl they will go into. If you accidentally spill, you might have way too much!

serves 4 to 6

preparation time: 15 minutes
cooking time: 15 minutes

ingredients:

¾ cup all-purpose flour
¾ cup whole wheat flour
½ cup quick oats
1 teaspoon salt
2 teaspoons baking powder
2 tablespoons brown sugar
1 teaspoon cinnamon
¾ cup soft raisins
2 large eggs
2 cups skim milk
3 tablespoons canola oil
1 teaspoon vanilla extract
maple syrup and butter or
    applesauce

equipment:

large mixing bowl
measuring cups—½ cup, ¼ cup
measuring spoons
whisk
medium mixing bowl
liquid measuring cup
wooden spoon
griddle or frying pan
ladle
spatula
serving plate

Oatmeal Raisin Pancakes

If you like oatmeal raisin cookies,
you'll love these pancakes. The sweet, chewy
raisins, oats, and whole wheat flour make
them a healthy breakfast treat.

1. In a large mixing bowl,
   combine all-purpose flour,
   whole wheat flour, quick oats,
   salt, baking powder, brown sugar,
   cinnamon, and raisins. **Blend**
   well with a whisk. Set aside.

2. **Crack** eggs into a medium
   mixing bowl. Use the whisk to
   whisk the eggs until combined.

3. **Add** skim milk, 2 tablespoons canola oil,
   and vanilla extract to eggs. **Stir** with the
   whisk to combine.

4. **Add** egg mixture to flour mixture. Use a wooden spoon to **mix** well.

5. **Place** the griddle or frying pan on the stove. Turn the burner under the griddle on medium, and **add** 1 tablespoon canola oil. Allow to warm for 2 minutes. **Place** the large mixing bowl right next to the griddle. Place a serving plate nearby too.

Turn the page for more Oatmeal Raisin Pancakes

6. Use a ladle to **scoop** the pancake batter, and **pour** it onto the griddle. Make a circle that is about 3 inches across. Repeat 2 to 3 more times to fill the griddle. Make sure to leave 1 to 2 inches between pancakes. That way, the pancakes won't run together.

7. **Cook** the pancakes for 1 to 2 minutes. Look for tiny air bubbles that form and pop all over the surface of the pancakes. That means it's time to flip the pancakes with a spatula. (Sometimes flipping takes practice. Ask an adult for help until you get the hang of it!)

8. **Cook** pancakes for 1 to 2 minutes on the second side. When done, the pancakes should be golden brown on both sides. Use the spatula to **place** the pancakes on the serving plate.

9. **Repeat** steps 6 through 8 until you've used all the batter. If the pancakes start to stick to the pan, add additional oil to the frying pan for each new batch of pancakes. Serve hot with maple syrup and butter or applesauce.

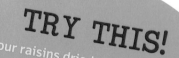

TRY THIS!

Are your raisins dried out? Soften them by soaking them in hot water. Heat 1 cup water in a small saucepan on the stove until it boils. Meanwhile, place the raisins in a liquid measuring cup. Ask an adult to pour the boiling water over the raisins. Let them soak for 10 minutes. Drain the water from the raisins into a colander placed in the kitchen sink. Add the raisins to your recipe according to directions.

Any soft, dried berries will work in this recipe. Try dried cranberries or cherries.

Sweet Potato Pancakes

These sweet, rich pancakes will warm you up on a crisp fall day.

1. In a large mixing bowl, **combine** all-purpose flour, whole wheat flour, salt, baking soda, brown sugar, and pie spice. **Blend** well with a whisk. Set aside.

Turn the page for more Sweet Potato Pancakes

serves 4 to 6

preparation time: 15 minutes
cooking time: 15 minutes

ingredients:
1 cup all-purpose flour
1 cup whole wheat flour
1 teaspoon salt
1 teaspoon baking soda
2 tablespoons brown sugar
½ teaspoon apple pie spice or pumpkin pie spice
2 eggs
2 cups buttermilk
3 tablespoons canola oil
1 cup canned sweet potato puree
maple syrup and butter

equipment:
large mixing bowl
measuring cups – 1 cup, ½ cup, ¼ cup
measuring spoons
whisk
medium mixing bowl
liquid measuring cup
can opener
wooden spoon
griddle or frying pan
ladle
spatula
serving plate

Sweet Potato Pancakes continued

2. **Crack** eggs into a medium mixing bowl. Use a whisk to **whisk** eggs until well combined.

3. **Add** buttermilk, 2 tablespoons canola oil, and sweet potato puree to eggs. **Stir** with the whisk to combine.

4. **Add** sweet potato mixture to flour mixture. Use the whisk to **mix** well. If the mixture becomes too thick for the whisk, switch to a wooden spoon.

5. **Place** the griddle or frying pan on the stove. Turn the burner under the griddle on medium, and **add** 1 tablespoon canola oil. Allow to warm for 2 minutes. **Place** the large mixing bowl right next to the griddle. Place the serving plate nearby too.

6. Use a ladle to **scoop** the pancake batter and **pour** it onto the griddle. Make a circle that is about 3 inches across. Repeat 2 to 3 more times to fill the griddle. Make sure to leave 1 to 2 inches between pancakes. That way, the pancakes won't run together.

7. **Cook** the pancakes for 1 to 2 minutes. Look for tiny air bubbles that form and pop all over the surface of the pancakes. That means it's time to flip the pancakes with a spatula. (Sometimes flipping takes practice. Ask an adult for help until you get the hang of it!)

8. **Cook** pancakes for 1 to 2 minutes on the second side. When done, the pancakes should be golden brown on both sides. Use the spatula to **place** the pancakes on the serving plate.

9. **Repeat** steps 6 through 8 until you've used all the batter. If the pancakes start to stick to the pan, add additional oil to the frying pan for each new batch of pancakes. Serve hot with maple syrup and butter.

TRY THIS!

If you cannot find sweet potato puree, make your own. (Do not use candied yams instead.) Peel and cut a medium sweet potato into ½-inch pieces. Place pieces in a bowl with ⅛ cup water, and microwave on high for 1½ minutes. Carefully remove from the microwave with the oven mitts. Check for doneness by sticking a fork into one of the pieces. The sweet potato should be very soft. If it's not, microwave it for another minute. Then drain the water and mash the sweet potato with the fork.

Use **pumpkin puree** instead of the sweet potato puree for a fun Halloween breakfast.

serves 4

preparation time: 15 minutes
cooking time: 20 minutes

ingredients:

1 ripe banana
2 eggs
2 cups skim milk
1½ cups whole wheat flour
⅓ cup plus 2 tablespoons
   canola oil
2 tablespoons honey
1 teaspoon flaxseeds
2 teaspoons baking powder
1¼ cups old-fashioned oats
maple syrup and butter

equipment:

waffle iron
2 small bowls
2 forks
blender
liquid measuring cup
measuring cups—1 cup,
   ½ cup, ¼ cup
measuring spoons
wooden spoon
pastry brush
serving plate

Banana Oat Waffles

These easy-to-make waffles are a perfect way
to use up ripe bananas.

1. Ask an adult to help you set up the waffle iron and show you how to use it. **Plug** it in, and let it warm up for 5 minutes before you make the waffles.

2. **Peel** the banana and break it into pieces. **Place** the banana pieces in a small bowl, and **mash** them with a fork.

3. **Crack** the eggs into the pitcher of a blender. **Add** whole wheat flour, ⅓ cup canola oil, mashed banana, honey, flaxseeds, and baking powder. **Put** the lid on the blender, and **blend** on high until the mixture is well mixed. Unplug the blender.

4. **Add** the oats to the blender. Use a wooden spoon to **stir** them in.

5. **Pour** 2 tablespoons canola oil into a small bowl. **Dip** a pastry brush into the oil. Then carefully **brush** a bit of the oil on the inside of the hot waffle iron. Be sure to **coat** the top and the bottom.

6. Use a ½-cup measuring cup to **scoop** a little less than ½ cup batter. Have an adult help you **pour** the batter into the center of the waffle iron. Close the waffle iron. **Bake** the waffle for about 5 minutes, or until golden brown. Many waffle irons have a light that goes on or off when the waffle is finished baking.

7. Carefully lift the lid of the waffle iron. Use a fork to **remove** the waffle, and **place** it on a serving plate.

8. **Repeat** steps 6 through 8 until you've used up all the batter. Serve waffles hot with butter and maple syrup.

TRY THIS!

Not a fan of bananas? Replace them with ¼ cup applesauce.

Add ½ cup chopped walnuts or pecans when you add the oats.

makes 18 muffins

preparation time: 20 minutes
baking time: 15 to 20 minutes

ingredients:

2 to 3 carrots
1 Granny Smith apple
1 cup all-purpose flour
1 cup whole wheat flour
2 teaspoons baking soda
2 teaspoons cinnamon
¼ teaspoon salt
1¼ cups sugar
½ cup raisins
½ cup sweetened shredded
 coconut
3 large eggs
⅓ cup plain low-fat yogurt
⅔ cup canola oil
2 teaspoons vanilla extract

equipment:

18 paper muffin liners
1 to 3 muffin tins
vegetable peeler
knife
cutting board
grater
measuring cups—1 cup,
 ½ cup, ⅓ cup, ¼ cup
large mixing bowl
measuring spoons
whisk
medium mixing bowl
liquid measuring cup
wooden spoon
ladle
rubber scraper
oven mitts
toothpicks
wire cooling rack

Favorite Carrot Muffins

These tasty muffins are yummy for breakfast with a glass of cold milk. Or have them as an after-school snack.

1. **Place** an oven rack in the center position in the oven. Then **preheat** the oven to 350°F. Place 18 paper muffin liners in muffin tins.

2. **Wash** the carrots and apple.

3. **Peel** the skin from the carrots with a vegetable peeler. Use a knife and a cutting board to **cut** off the stem and tip of each carrot. Then use a grater to **grate** the carrots over the cutting board. Grate enough to measure 2 cups. Set aside.

4. To cut the apple, first **cut** it in half from top to bottom on the cutting board. Cut the first half in half again from top to bottom. Then cut out and **discard** the stem and seeds. Repeat with the second half. Then **grate** the apple pieces—skin and all—over the cutting board. Grate enough to measure ½ cup. Set aside.

5. In a large mixing bowl, **combine** all-purpose flour, whole wheat flour, baking soda, cinnamon, salt, and sugar. Use a whisk to **blend** well.

6. **Add** the grated carrots, raisins, and shredded coconut to the flour mixture. **Stir** with the whisk to mix well.

7. One at a time, **crack** the eggs into a medium mixing bowl. **Add** plain low-fat yogurt, canola oil, and vanilla extract. **Whisk** with the whisk until well mixed. **Add** the grated apple to the egg mixture, and **stir** with the whisk.

Turn the page for more Favorite Carrot Muffins

8. **Add** the egg mixture to the flour mixture. **Stir** with a wooden spoon until the flour mixture is just blended with the egg mixture. Do not overmix.

9. **Place** the large mixing bowl right next to the muffin tin. Use a ladle to **scoop** and **pour** some batter into one of the prepared muffin cups. **Fill** the cup two-thirds full. Repeat until you have used up all the batter. (Use a rubber scraper to get out the last bit of batter.)

10. Use oven mitts to **place** the muffin tins on the center rack in the oven. **Bake** for 15 minutes, or until done. To check for doneness, use oven mitts to **remove** a muffin tin. **Stick** a toothpick straight down into the center of a muffin. If the toothpick comes out clean, the muffins are done. If pieces of muffin cling to the toothpick, bake the muffins for 2 to 3 more minutes. Then test them again. Repeat as needed.

11. Use oven mitts to **remove** the muffin tins from the oven. **Place** the tins on a wire cooling rack to cool for 5 minutes. Carefully **remove** muffins from the warm tins with a fork. Then place them on the wire rack to cool completely.

TRY THIS!

Replace the grated apple with 1 small grated zucchini.

Add ½ cup chopped walnuts or pecans to the flour mixture when you add the carrots.

Gooey Caramel Rolls

Impress your family with these yummy rolls. Your family won't believe how simple these rolls were to make!

makes 12 to 15 large rolls

preparation time: 10 minutes
rising time: 8 hours or overnight
baking time: 25 minutes

ingredients
½ cup (1 stick) unsalted butter
½ cup brown sugar
1 teaspoon vanilla extract
½ teaspoon salt
½ teaspoon cinnamon
½ cup raisins or
chopped pecans
½ package frozen dinner roll
dough balls, such as
Rhodes Rolls
½ package butterscotch
pudding mix (3.4-ounce box
cook and serve, not instant)

equipment
Bundt cake pan or
2 deep loaf pans
medium saucepan
measuring cup—½ cup
measuring spoons
wooden spoon
rubber scraper
clean dish towel
(not terry cloth)
oven mitts
1 or 2 large serving plates

1. **Unwrap** the stick of butter halfway, and hold the wrapper-covered end. Use the stick of butter to completely **grease** the entire inside of a Bundt cake pan or 2 loaf pans.

2. **Place** the rest of the butter in a medium saucepan. **Add** brown sugar, vanilla extract, salt, and cinnamon. (Be sure to pack the brown sugar tightly into the measuring cup before adding.)

Turn the page for more Gooey Caramel Rolls

3. Turn the burner under the saucepan on medium. **Melt** the butter with the other ingredients, stirring often with a wooden spoon. Bring the mixture to a boil. **Boil** for 1 minute. Then turn off the burner and **remove** the saucepan.

4. **Sprinkle** raisins or nuts in the bottom of the Bundt pan or the 2 loaf pans. **Pour** half of the melted butter mixture into the bottom of the pan(s) to cover the raisins or nuts. Set aside the other half of the butter mixture.

5. **Open** the package of frozen dough balls. **Place** the dough balls on their side along the bottom of the pan(s). **Put** the balls side by side to fill the entire bottom of the pan(s).

6. **Open** the package of butterscotch pudding mix. **Sprinkle** half of it evenly over the top of all the dough balls. **Pour** the remaining melted butter mixture evenly over the top of the dough balls. Use a rubber scraper to get out all the butter mixture.

7. **Wet** a dish towel with warm water to dampen it. Wring out the towel, and use it to **cover** the top of the pan(s). Allow the dough to **rise** in a warm place for 8 hours or overnight.

8. When you are ready to bake, **place** an oven rack in the center position in the oven. **Preheat** the oven to 350°F.

9. Uncover the pan(s), and use oven mitts to **place** the rolls in the oven. **Bake** for 25 minutes, or until golden brown. Use oven mitts to **remove** the hot pan(s) from the oven. **Place** the pan(s) on top of the stove.

10. **Place** a serving plate upside down over the top of each pan. Ask an adult to help carefully **flip** each pan. The pan will be on top and the plate on the bottom. Carefully lift the pan with oven mitts. You may need to **shake** the pan slightly to free the sticky rolls from the pan's sides. These rolls are best warm, so serve immediately.

TRY THIS!

To make orange-cinnamon rolls, add 3 tablespoons thawed orange juice concentrate to the brown sugar mixture. Leave out the salt and raisins or pecans. Use half a package of vanilla pudding mix instead of butterscotch pudding.

To make lemon and cardamom rolls, add 3 tablespoons thawed lemonade concentrate to the brown sugar mixture. Leave out the salt and raisins or nuts. Replace the cinnamon with ¼ teaspoon ground cardamom. Use half a package of lemon pudding mix instead of butterscotch pudding.

makes 8 croissants

preparation time: 10 minutes
baking time: 10 minutes

ingredients

1 tube crescent rolls
½ cup dark or semisweet
  chocolate chips
¼ cup powdered sugar

equipment

1 cookie sheet
measuring cups—½ cup,
  ¼ cup
measuring spoons
oven mitts
spatula
small mesh strainer
serving plate

Chocolaty Croissants

These croissants are as easy to make as they are
to eat. Dust them with a little powdered sugar.
They'll look like they came straight from the bakery!

1. **Place** an oven rack in the center position of
   the oven. Then **preheat** the oven to 350°F.

2. **Open** the crescent rolls by
   following the directions on the
   package. **Unroll** triangles of
   dough. **Place** them in rows
   on a cookie sheet. Leave 1 to 2
   inches between each triangle.

3. **Sprinkle** 1 tablespoon of chocolate
   chips in the center of each triangle.

4. With your fingers, **lift** the wide base of a triangle.
   Carefully **roll** the triangle toward the tip to make a
   tube. Repeat with the other triangles.

5. Use oven mitts to **place** the cookie sheet on the center rack in the oven. **Bake** for 10 minutes, or until golden brown. Use oven mitts to **remove** the cookie sheet from the oven. Use a spatula to **place** the croissants on a serving plate.

6. Hold a small mesh strainer over the croissants. **Add** the powdered sugar to the strainer, and **shake** it gently over the top of each croissant. Use enough sugar to lightly dust each croissant. **Serve** immediately. Once cool, the chocolate hardens.

TRY THIS!

Replace the chocolate chips with canned **apple pie filling** or your favorite **jam**. Drop 1 tablespoon of the filling or jam on each croissant triangle before rolling.

serves 4 to 6

preparation time: 20 minutes
first rise: 2 hours
resting time: 2 hours or overnight
second rise: 45 minutes
baking time: 30 minutes

ingredients:

1½ cups water
1½ teaspoons salt
1 package (2¼ teaspoons) active
   dry yeast
¼ cup honey
3 plus ¼ cups all-purpose flour
¼ cup whole wheat flour
2 tablespoons cornmeal

equipment:

2-cup liquid measuring cup
food thermometer (optional)
large mixing bowl
measuring spoons
measuring cups—1 cup, ¼ cup
whisk
wooden spoon
clean dish towel
cookie sheet
oven mitts
wire cooling rack

Easy Honey Wheat Bread

It's much easier than you think to make fresh, homemade bread. This delicious recipe is perfect for beginners. Just plan ahead for the rising and resting time.

1. **Fill** a liquid measuring cup with 1½ cups water. **Heat** it in the microwave on high for 20 seconds. Remove the water from the microwave. Stick a finger in the water, and dab it on the inside of your wrist. The water should feel a little warm, but *not* hot. Hot water will kill the yeast. (If you have a food thermometer, you can use it to check the temperature of the water. It should be between 105°F and 115°F.)

2. In a large mixing bowl, **combine** the warm water, salt, yeast, and honey. **Stir** well with a whisk.

3. **Add** 3 cups all-purpose flour and whole wheat flour to the water and yeast mixture. **Stir** with a wooden spoon to mix well. If the dough gets too hard to stir, use your hands instead. Put some flour on your hands first to keep them from sticking to the dough.

4. **Wet** a dish towel with warm water to dampen it. Wring out the towel, and use it to cover the bowl. **Place** the bowl in a warm area in your kitchen. Allow the dough to **rise** for 2 hours, or until it has doubled in size.

Turn the page for more Easy Honey Wheat Bread

TRY THIS!

Add ½ cup soft **raisins** and ½ teaspoon **cinnamon** when you add the flour.

This bread can be made with all white flour, if you prefer.

5. After the dough has risen, **place** the covered bowl of dough in the refrigerator for at least 2 hours or overnight. (Cool dough is easier to work with).

6. On baking day, **remove** the bowl of dough from the refrigerator. **Sprinkle** the cornmeal onto a cookie sheet. Use your hand to **spread** the cornmeal around in a circle in the center of the cookie sheet.

7. **Remove** the towel from the bowl. **Sprinkle** ¼ cup all-purpose flour over the entire surface of the dough, dusting a little on your hands as well.

8. **Grab** the dough on either side and lift it up. Use your hands to quickly **shape** it into a smooth mound. **Tuck** the stray edges of dough under the mound. This is your loaf.

9. **Place** the loaf rounded side up on top of the circle of cornmeal you made. Then set the cookie sheet in a warm place. Allow the loaf to **rise** uncovered for 45 minutes.

10. **Place** an oven rack in the center of the oven. Then **preheat** the oven to 450°F.

11. Have an adult **score** a plus sign on the top of the loaf with a sharp bread knife.

12. Use oven mitts to **place** the cookie sheet on the center rack in the oven. **Bake** the bread for 30 minutes, or until golden brown. Use oven mitts to **remove** the bread from the oven. Place the bread on a wire cooling rack. Allow it to cool for 1 hour before slicing.

serves 8 to 2

preparation time: 15 minutes
baking time: 50 to 55 minutes

ingredients:

1 tablespoon plus ⅓ cup canola
  oil
1 cup all-purpose flour
1 cup whole wheat flour
2 teaspoons cinnamon
¼ teaspoon nutmeg
¼ teaspoon ginger
2 teaspoons baking soda
½ teaspoon salt
2 eggs
¼ cup plain low-fat yogurt
¼ cup applesauce
1 cup brown sugar
2 teaspoons vanilla extract
2 medium zucchini
½ cup dark chocolate chips
½ cup soft raisins

equipment:

loaf pan
paper towels
large mixing bowl
measuring cups—1 cup, ½ cup
measuring spoons
whisk
medium mixing bowl
liquid measuring cup
cutting board
knife
grater
wooden spoon
rubber scraper
toothpicks
oven mitts
wire cooling rack

28

Yummy Zucchini Bread

Make this tasty breakfast bread in late summer,
when zucchini is widely available.

1. **Place** an oven rack in the center position in the
   oven. Then **preheat** the oven to 350°F.

2. **Pour** 1 tablespoon canola oil into the bottom
   of a loaf pan. Use a paper towel to **grease** the
   corners, sides, and bottom of the pan with the oil.

3. In a large mixing bowl, **combine**
   all-purpose flour, whole wheat
   flour, cinnamon, nutmeg, ginger,
   baking soda, and salt. Use a whisk
   to **mix** well.

4. **Crack** the eggs into a medium
   mixing bowl. Use the whisk to
   whisk the eggs until the yolks and
   whites are well blended. **Add** ⅓ cup
   canola oil, yogurt, applesauce, brown
   sugar, and vanilla extract. (Be sure to
   pack the brown sugar tightly into the
   measuring cup before adding.) Use
   the whisk to **blend** well.

5. **Wash** the zucchini in cool water, and pat dry. Use a knife and a cutting board to **slice** off the ends of each zucchini. With a grater, **grate** the zucchini over the cutting board. Grate enough to measure 1½ cups. **Add** the grated zucchini to the egg mixture. **Stir** well with the whisk.

Turn the page for more Yummy Zucchini Bread

TRY THIS!

For a slightly sweeter bread, replace the plain yogurt with **vanilla yogurt**.

Turn this into a banana bread recipe by replacing the shredded zucchini with 2 mashed, ripe **bananas**.

Leave out the chocolate chips and/or raisins.

Add ½ cup chopped **walnuts** or **pecans**.

6. **Add** the egg mixture to the flour mixture. **Stir** with the wooden spoon to mix. **Add** dark chocolate chips and raisins to the batter. **Stir** again to mix.

7. **Pour** the batter into the prepared loaf pan. Use the rubber scraper to **scrape** all the batter from the mixing bowl.

8. Use oven mitts to **place** the loaf pan on the center rack in the oven. **Bake** for 50 to 55 minutes, or until done. To check for doneness, use oven mitts to **remove** the loaf pan from the oven. **Stick** a toothpick straight down into the center of a loaf. If the toothpick comes out clean, the bread is done. If pieces of bread cling to the toothpick, bake the bread for 2 to 3 more minutes. Then test it again. Repeat as needed.

9. **Place** the loaf pan on the wire cooling rack. Allow to cool for 10 minutes. Then have an adult help you turn the loaf out of the pan. **Slice** when completely cool, after about 30 minutes.

SPECIAL INGREDIENTS

apple pie or pumpkin pie spice: a mix of cinnamon, nutmeg, allspice, ginger, cardamom, and cloves. Pie spice is sold in the spice section of most grocery stores.

cardamom: an Indian spice made from the small seeds that grow inside cardamom pods. It can be found in the spice section of most grocery stores.

coarse sugar: coarsely ground sugar used to add a slightly sweet decoration to the top of baked foods. Look for it in the baking section of most grocery stores.

crescent rolls: ready-made dough packaged in a cardboard tube. It can be found in the refrigerator section of the grocery store.

dinner roll dough: ready-made balls of dinner roll dough. They can be found in the frozen foods section of most grocery stores. Look for small-sized dinner roll balls that are sold in plastic bags. Do not buy the already-formed rolls in aluminum tins.

flaxseeds: small brown or golden seeds from the flax plant that are often used in bread baking. Look for flaxseeds in the bulk section or health food section of your grocery store or food co-op.

oats: a type of grain that comes from the oat plant. Old-fashioned oats take longer to cook but add more texture to foods. Quick oats cook faster and are better for some baking recipes. Both types of oats can be found in the cereal aisle of the grocery store.

pumpkin puree: mashed pumpkin sold in cans in the canned vegetable section or baking section of most grocery stores

sweetened shredded coconut: the shredded white insides of a coconut. Sweetened shredded coconut is sold in bags in the baking aisle of most grocery stores.

sweet potato puree: mashed sweet potatoes sold in the canned vegetable section of most grocery stores

vanilla extract: liquid vanilla flavor. You can find vanilla in the baking aisle of the grocery store. Most stores sell both pure vanilla extract and artificially flavored extract. Either type will work.

whole wheat flour: flour made by grinding and using all the wheat grain. Whole wheat flour is located in the baking aisle of the grocery store.

FURTHER READING AND WEBSITES

Choose My Plate
http://www.choosemyplate.gov
/children-over-five.html
Download coloring pages, play an interactive computer game, and get lots of nutrition information at this U.S. Department of Agriculture website.

Farmers Markets Search
http://apps.ams.usda.gov/FarmersMarkets/
Visit this site to find a farmers' market near you!

Graimes, Nicola. *Kids' Fun and Healthy Cookbook.* New York: DK, 2007. This recipe-packed cookbook has a chapter on baking muffins, breads, and rolls.

Nissenberg, Sandra. *The Everything Kids' Cookbook: From Mac 'n Cheese to Double Chocolate Chip Cookies — 90 Recipes to Have Some Finger-Lickin' Fun.* Avon, MA: Adams Media, 2008.
This cookbook is a great source for recipes kids love to make, including recipes for muffins and breads.

Recipes
http://www.sproutonline.com
/crafts-and-recipes/recipes
Find more fun and easy recipes for kids at this site.

INDEX

You're the Chef
Metric Conversions

VOLUME

⅛ teaspoon	0.62 milliliters
¼ teaspoon	1.2 milliliters
½ teaspoon	2.5 milliliters
¾ teaspoon	3.7 milliliters
1 teaspoon	5 milliliters
½ tablespoon	7.4 milliliters
1 tablespoon	15 milliliters
⅛ cup	30 milliliters
¼ cup	59 milliliters
⅓ cup	79 milliliters
½ cup	118 milliliters
⅔ cup	158 milliliters
¾ cup	177 milliliters
1 cup	237 milliliters
2 quarts (8 cups)	1,893 milliliters
3 fluid ounces	89 milliliters
12 fluid ounces	355 milliliters
24 fluid ounces	710 milliliters

MASS (weight)

1 ounce	28 grams
3.4 ounces	96 grams
3.5 ounces	99 grams
4 ounces	113 grams
7 ounces	198 grams
8 ounces	227 grams
12 ounces	340 grams
14.5 ounces	411 grams
15 ounces	425 grams
15.25 ounces	432 grams
16 ounces (1 pound)	454 grams
17 ounces	482 grams
21 ounces	595 grams

TEMPERATURE

Fahrenheit	Celsius
170°	77°
185°	85°
250°	121°
325°	163°
350°	177°
375°	191°
400°	204°
425°	218°
450°	232°

LENGTH

¼ inch	0.6 centimeters
½ inch	1.27 centimeters
1 inch	2.5 centimeters
2 inches	5 centimeters
3 inches	7.6 centimeters
5 inches	13 centimeters
8 inches	20 centimeters
9 x 11 inches	23 x 28 centimeters
9 x 13 inches	23 x 33 centimeters